MY REAL ESTATE JOURNEY

How I transitioned from being an insurance marketer to a thriving real estate entrepreneur

PEACE UKAMAKA

My Real Estate Journey

Copyright 2024© Peace Ukamaka

All rights reserved.

No part of this book may be reproduced or transmitted in any form, or by any means, including photocopying, recording, or other electronic or mechanical methods, without the prior written permission of the publisher, except in the case of a brief quotation embodied in critical reviews and specific other non-commercial uses permitted by copyright laws. All translations of this work must be approved in writing by the publisher.

ISBN: 9798342848107

ACKNOWLEDGMENTS

I begin by expressing my deepest gratitude to God Almighty for His protection, guidance, and provision throughout this journey. I am thankful for the gift of the incredible people who have supported and inspired me along the way.

First and foremost, I extend my heartfelt thanks to my beloved children—Blessed Chinwekele, Pearl Oluomachi, and Amazingrace Oluebubechukwu. You are my greatest motivation and the reason I continue to push forward and never give up.

I would like to express my sincere gratitude to my mentors:

- **Engr. Gabin Iyoha**, for his belief in my vision and invaluable guidance.
- **Dr. Christopher Onolaja**, the GMD of Revolution Plus, for his mentorship and support during the later stages of my business and beyond.

A special thank you to my colleagues:

- **Amb. Chris Emodi** and **Dr. Femi Oshofowora**, for the continuous spirit of collaboration and support as we grow together.

- **Dr. Jennifer Saidu**, my big sister and greatest cheerleader, for her encouragement and belief in me, and for reviewing this book with such care and insight.

I am also immensely grateful to my team at Trusted Choice Assets:

- **Cletus Dumbiri**, the Dean at the Nigerian Training Institute for Real Estate Entrepreneurs,
- **Chiamaka Ubani**, the HR at Trusted Choice Assets,
- **Sulaimon Alfred Paul**, the CFO at Trusted Choice Assets,
- And all other staff members at both Trusted Choice Assets and the Nigerian Training Institute for Real Estate Entrepreneurs.

My spiritual journey has been guided by:

- **Rev. Sunny Ikwa Itomo**, my spiritual father and company clergy, who has supported me for almost a decade,
- **Apostle Lawrence Onochie**, my pastor at The Kings Heritage, who provided divine direction on overhauling my business.

To my readers, thank you for your interest in my story. I hope that my experiences and lessons learned will provide valuable insights and inspire you on your own journey.

Finally, I am grateful to everyone who has contributed, directly or indirectly, to the completion of this book. Your support has made this endeavor possible, and I am truly appreciative.

With deep gratitude.

Table of Contents

ACKNOWLEDGMENTS 3

INTRODUCTION 9

Chapter One 11

   THE BEGINNING: THE SPARK OF INSPIRATION 11

CHAPTER TWO 20

   FIRST STEPS 20

CHAPTER THREE 37

   STARTING/ BUILDING MY BUSINESS 37

CHAPTER FOUR 51

   LESSONS LEARNED SO FAR 51

CHAPTER FIVE 61

   KEEPING UP THE PACE 61

CONCLUSION 79

ABOUT THE AUTHOR 83

INTRODUCTION

My Real Estate Journey

Welcome to "My Real Estate Journey," This book highlights the story of how I transitioned from being an insurance marketer to a thriving real estate entrepreneur. My adventure in real estate began during my time at African Alliance Insurance PLC, a period that was both challenging and enlightening. In this book, I candidly recount the mistakes I made, the lessons I learned, and the successes I achieved along the way. My story is a testament to perseverance, growth, and continuous progress in the dynamic world of real estate. I hope that by sharing my experiences, I can offer valuable insights and inspire others who are embarking on their own real estate journeys and in any other business.

Chapter One

THE BEGINNING: THE SPARK OF INSPIRATION

One fateful afternoon, as I was out in the field scouting for new insurance customers, something unusual happened that would change my life forever. Unlike my typical routine of visiting bustling marketplaces or offices through referrals, I found myself at Town Planning Way in

Ilupeju, where my insurance company's office was located. After a productive meeting with my manager and submitting all the required reports, I decided to stop by a nearby branch of GTBank, also on Town Planning Way in Lagos.

While in the banking hall, I noticed an elderly man struggling with his transfer form. Instinctively, I approached him and offered to help. As I filled out the form on his behalf, he revealed that he intended to transfer a substantial amount—two million naira—to another account. Seeing the significant sum, a thought crossed my mind: "Peace, this man has money. You need to sell something to him."

After the transaction was completed, I introduced myself and began prospecting him, hoping to either sell to him a soft insurance policy or secure a referral from him. To my surprise, the elderly man responded with unexpected advice. He said, "Peace, I like you. You're a great salesperson with a lot of empathy. You would excel even more in a different industry." Curious, I asked, "Different? In what industry, please?" He replied, "You would make it big in the real estate industry."

At that time, in 2019, the term "Real Estate" was completely new to me. I had never really paid attention to it or considered it as an industry I want to play in or as a career path. Despite my initial skepticism, the word "Real Estate" lingered in my mind and became a persistent source of intrigue, keeping me awake almost all nights. Determined to understand what it was all about, I immersed myself in research. I scoured Google, seeking answers to my questions about real estate and how I could become involved and sell better in this industry that seemed poised to transform my life.

My curiosity grew so intense that it kept me away from my insurance marketing duties for an entire week. I was consumed by a desire to grasp the fundamentals of real estate and explore this new venture. Then, one afternoon, while resuming my usual marketing activities, I encountered another pivotal moment. I boarded a car heading towards my destination, I noticed a young man wearing a shirt emblazoned with a house logo. Seizing the opportunity, I asked him if he was real estate agent, and when he confirmed he was, I eagerly requested that he teaches me about it.

This chance encounter marked the beginning of my journey into real estate industry. Little did I know that this initial spark of curiosity and the advice of a stranger would ignite a passion that would guide me through the ups and downs of an entirely new industry.

Following my initial encounter with the young man in the car, I took a significant step toward exploring the world of real estate. Mr. Jonathan, who had been kind enough to engage with me, invited me to his office located at Gowon Estate, Egbeda. I eagerly accepted the invitation, hoping to gain more insight into this intriguing industry.

Upon arriving at Mr. Jonathan's office, I was greeted by what appeared to be a seminar in progress. The office belonged to Oxford Commercial Services, a company that specialized in properties primarily located in Ogun State and was heavily involved in agriculture. The presentation was comprehensive, but to be honest, much of it went over my head during that first visit. The jargon and specifics of the real estate and agricultural sectors were new and confusing to me.

Determined to understand more, I continued my online research and made additional visits to Oxford Commercial Services on subsequent occasions. Each visit provided me with more information, though I still struggled to grasp all the concepts. Nevertheless, my curiosity and dedication kept me going.

One profound observation I made during this early phase was the way the universe seemed to align with my newfound interest. It was as if once I set my mind on real estate, opportunities and resources began to present themselves to me. I started noticing flyers, advertisements, and people actively marketing real estate. It felt as though these signs had always been around, but I had never paid them any attention until now.

This newfound awareness was both exciting and overwhelming. I realized that my focus on real estate was drawing the very people and information I needed to deepen my understanding of the industry. It became clear to me that my journey was guided by a combination of curiosity, persistence, and perhaps a touch of serendipity. Each step I took, each person I met, and each piece of information I uncovered was bringing me closer to unraveling the mysteries of real estate and charting my path forward in this transformative field.

As I delved deeper into understanding the concepts, products, and services at Oxford Commercial Services, I also sought spiritual guidance to ensure that my journey into real estate was aligned with my purpose. It was during this phase that Shola, a colleague at Oxford, introduced me to a WhatsApp group with over 2,000 realtors. This group was dedicated to marketing properties from various real estate companies. Despite being a novice, I joined the group with unwavering confidence, convinced that my foray into real estate was destined for success.

One day, I received an email from the BRG group announcing the unveiling of a new real estate company. The excitement of this news was palpable, and I felt an irresistible urge to attend the event. I invited my friends Blessing Ogbobe and Bode George, who traveled all the way from Ilorin to join me. I have always had a knack for convincing people to embrace opportunities I believe in, and this event was no exception. My enthusiasm for real estate and the potential I saw in it drove me to share this experience with those close to me.

The unveiling event, held in 2019, was a significant milestone. The new real estate company introduced was named OGA FOR PROPERTIES, which later became known as ZYLUS HOMES AND PROPERTIES. This event marked another pivotal moment in my journey, reinforcing my belief in the potential of the real estate industry and further solidifying my commitment to pursuing a career in this field.

Throughout this journey, I have been guided not only by my curiosity and determination but also by a sense of divine direction. It became evident that my path was being shaped by both my efforts and the spiritual support I sought, ensuring that I remained focused and driven as I navigated the complexities of the real estate world.

CHAPTER TWO

FIRST STEPS

Embarking on a new career in real estate was filled with both excitement and uncertainty. My initial foray into the industry was under the auspices of OGA FOR PROPERTY, facilitated by the BRG Realtor group. My decision to focus on this new venture was influenced by several critical factors, including the leadership at OGA FOR PROPERTY. The Managing Director, who also had a background in insurance marketing like myself, assured me of his commitment to integrity and security—values that resonated deeply with me.

However, despite this alignment in values, I still harbored some confusion about which company to commit to, as Oxford Commercial Services offered similar products. Seeking clarity and reassurance, I turned to my spiritual guide, Pastor Sunny Ikwa Itomo. After sharing my aspirations and the opportunities before me, he prayed with me and encouraged me to proceed, affirming that God's support was with me.

Buoyed by this spiritual affirmation, I made a silent prayer to God as I left the meeting. I vowed that if God granted me my first sale in this industry, I would dedicate the entire commission to my spiritual father, a vow I kept secret. Almost immediately after making this vow, an intriguing opportunity presented itself. A lady reached out to me, interested in investing 1.5 million naira in Oxford's agricultural projects. I saw this as a perfect moment to steer her towards investing in land banking with OGA FOR PROPERTY instead.

Amidst our conversation, my spiritual father unexpectedly called, asking me to visit him the following day. During this visit, he surprised me by gifting me 250,000 naira to support my new venture. His generosity overwhelmed me, and I took it as a divine sign that I was on the right path. This amount, though significant, was less than the minimum investment required at OGA FOR PROPERTY, which was one million naira, while Oxford accepted investments as low as 100,000 naira. Despite this, my conviction led me to OGA FOR PROPERTY's office in Allen, Ikeja.

Initially, their accountant hesitated to accept the 250,000 naira because it fell below the usual minimum investment. However, after consulting with the boss, they agreed to accept it. This transaction was officially recorded as my first sale in the real estate sector—a milestone that not only marked my entry into this industry but also reinforced my belief that my path was divinely guided.

This experience taught me the power of faith and persistence. It showed me that with determination, spiritual alignment, and the right network, one could overcome the initial hurdles of entering a new industry. It was a testament to the fact that sometimes, the smallest steps can lead to significant milestones on the journey to success.

After securing my first sale in real estate, I was emboldened to extend my efforts to social media platforms like Facebook, WhatsApp, and Instagram. This exposure brought a mix of reactions from different quarters. Some people accused me of engaging in fraudulent activities, commonly referred to as "419" in Nigeria, due to the rampant scams associated with high-value transactions. Others congratulated me, perceiving my entry into the real estate sector as a ticket into the "millionaire club," given the common belief that realtors often make substantial incomes. A few cautioned me about the risks involved, warning that poor decisions in real estate could lead to serious legal troubles, even jail.

Amid these varied reactions, some saw an opportunity to leverage my newfound enthusiasm for their benefit. It was during this phase that a secondary school mate, Mr. Martins Idudu, approached me with a proposal to sell a landed property in Ayobo belonging to one Alhaji. Eager to expand my portfolio and capitalize on this chance, I accepted the challenge without much consideration of the potential complexities involved.

As a novice, my focus was singular: sell the property quickly and earn a commission. I visited the site, recorded videos, and aggressively marketed the land across my social media platforms. Soon, a woman from my church expressed interest on behalf of another church member. The property was priced at 1,200,000 naira, and after showcasing the land to the interested buyer, he decided to purchase and paid in full. However, a significant oversight became apparent—he refused to pay me a commission, arguing that it had never been mentioned at the outset.

This incident was a stark lesson in the importance of clear communication in real estate transactions. Moreover, it highlighted an even more crucial aspect I had overlooked: due diligence. It later emerged that the land was located in a swampy area, a fact I had not verified before making the sale. Consequently, the buyer had to undertake the additional expenses of rectifying the property's documentation with the government and extensive sand filling to prepare the site for construction.

My first land sale was, undeniably, a disaster in terms of customer satisfaction. While I had succeeded in making money, I had failed to ensure a beneficial transaction for my client. This experience taught me that success in real estate isn't just about closing deals; it's about closing deals that are advantageous and satisfactory to all parties involved. It underscored the necessity of due diligence and proper communication, lessons that were vital for my growth and integrity as a real estate professional.

Learning from the setbacks of my initial land sale, I dedicated myself to gaining deeper knowledge and expertise in the real estate industry. I sought out educational resources, enrolling in online courses and gathering materials that could provide a thorough understanding of the sector. My quest for advancement led me to join PWAN (Property World African Network), one of Nigeria's pioneering real estate companies known for its network marketing approach to property sales.

Being part of the PWAN community opened up new avenues for professional development. I had the opportunity to attend various events and engage in weekly training sessions that were instrumental in honing my skills. Inspired by my background in the insurance industry, I began to adapt and apply similar skills to real estate. I crafted proposals aimed at companies, churches, cooperatives, and banks, encouraging them to invest in estate properties. Alongside my team leaders and colleagues, I delivered presentations to these organizations, effectively communicating the value and potential returns of real estate investments.

The efforts paid off significantly. I facilitated major sales for Oga for Property, and my friend Blessing Ogbobe, whom I had brought into the fold, also succeeded in making sales. My network expanded as I continued to secure deals for PWAN and concurrently grew my own team of real estate professionals. It seemed as though my career was on a rapid upward trajectory—until the unexpected happened: the onset of COVID-19.

The pandemic brought unprecedented challenges and disruptions across all sectors, including real estate. The impact was immediate and profound, affecting the way we conducted business, interacted with clients, and pursued new opportunities.

The advent of the COVID-19 pandemic marked a turning point in many sectors worldwide, and the impact was profoundly felt in the insurance industry, which struggled with numerous claims and other operational challenges. However, in stark contrast, the real estate sector experienced a surge in activity. Many investors recognized the unique opportunities that crises present, particularly in the property market, where prices during such times are often much lower than they are likely to be in the aftermath.

During this period, I leveraged the digital marketing skills I had honed—utilizing platforms like WhatsApp and Facebook to effectively promote my real estate offerings. This strategy proved immensely successful, allowing me to continue making sales despite the widespread disruptions and economic uncertainties.

Interestingly, it became clear that many people were eager to invest in real estate during the pandemic, understanding the long-term value of acquiring property at crisis-driven prices. This insight into investor psychology during crises was a crucial lesson for me. It reinforced the importance of being adaptable and responsive to market conditions, turning potential challenges into opportunities.

Amid the pandemic, I managed to sell two acres of land in the rapidly developing area of Ibeju Lekki, a testament to the robust demand for real estate in strategically chosen locations. Furthermore, one of my team members succeeded in selling three acres, underscoring the collective success of our strategies and the resilience of the real estate market even in difficult times.

This phase of my journey not only underscored the resilience required to navigate through such unprecedented challenges but also highlighted the potential for significant growth in the face of adversity. The pandemic taught me that with the right approach and understanding of market dynamics, one could not only survive but thrive, expanding one's portfolio and building lasting relationships with clients who trust your expertise and commitment to their investment needs.

As the world began to recover from the lockdowns imposed due to the COVID-19 pandemic, the real estate market started to regain its momentum. It was during this period of transition that I encountered an opportunity that significantly enhanced my understanding of the real estate business, especially when dealing with properties located outside of planned developments.

Juliet Akwari, a former classmate, reached out to inform me that her brother, residing in the UK, was interested in purchasing an acre of land behind The Redeemed Camp in Shimawa. This request marked my first venture into land scouting—a stark departure from my usual practice of marketing available listings. Unlike my previous experience with the Ayobo property, I approached this task with a commitment to thoroughness and due diligence. I was determined to ensure that the land was free from any government encumbrances, verified the root title, and confirmed that the land was dry.

After completing all necessary checks and confirming the land's suitability, the client proceeded with the purchase. This time, both the client and the owner of the property paid commissions, a testament to the effectiveness of clear and precise communication from the onset of the transaction.

Aware of the complications that could arise from purchasing land owned by a family or community, I advised the client to register the land with the government promptly. Despite my advice, the client hesitated to take the necessary steps. Seven months later, the owner of the property died, and I immediately contacted the client to recommend fencing the property to establish clear ownership boundaries. This action was crucial to prevent any potential disputes with the deceased family members, who might claim ownership or contest the sale.

Unfortunately, the client's initial reluctance to secure the property legally and physically led to complications that required my intervention to help resolve the emerging disputes. This experience highlighted one of the significant disadvantages of selling property not located within an estate: the need for immediate and proactive measures to secure one's investment.

Reflecting on this transaction, I decided to focus my efforts on selling properties within estates. This approach would minimize the risks associated with land ownership disputes and provide a more structured and secure investment environment for my clients. This shift not only aligned with my commitment to ensuring client satisfaction but also helped in fostering a reputation for reliable and professional real estate services.

In the upcoming chapter, we will explore the significant evolution of my career from a budding real estate agent to a multifaceted industry leader. This part of my journey details how I transitioned into a licensed and professional real estate consultant, an influential developer, a dedicated real estate sales coach, and a successful CEO of a burgeoning company.

The transformation involved not only expanding my knowledge and skills but also scaling my operations to manage a dynamic team. As my expertise deepened, I recognized the potential to influence the real estate sector more broadly. This realization prompted me to establish a company with a staff strength of over 15 dedicated professionals, each contributing to the vision of delivering exceptional real estate solutions to our clients.

We will delve into the strategies that facilitated this growth, the challenges I faced while scaling operations, and the lessons learned in leadership and business management. This chapter will also highlight how I leveraged my experiences to mentor others in the industry, fostering a culture of excellence and integrity within my team and the broader real estate community.

CHAPTER THREE

STARTING/ BUILDING MY BUSINESS

In June 2020, amidst a global pandemic that shook the foundations of many industries, I made a strategic decision to reach out to Pascal Property, proposing to join their organization as an exclusive salesperson. This decision was driven by a realization that significant learning and career progression in real estate would require focused effort and dedication within a single organization. It was important for me to consolidate my experiences and achievements in one place, as I aspired to eventually lead my own real estate company.

By August 2020, I officially joined Pascal Property as a Branch Coordinator of Sales, located at their Allen Ikeja office—the same place where I made my first successful transaction the previous year. My role involved a variety of responsibilities, but primarily, I focused on building and leading a team. I utilized Facebook and local recruitment agents to attract marketers, conducting interviews and training sessions every Tuesday at the office. The company had also expanded by opening another office at Sangotedo on the island in Lagos.

As a Branch Coordinator, I attended coordinators' meetings every Monday at 10 AM. Living on the mainland in Ijaye Abule-Egba meant I had to leave my house by 5 AM to ensure I arrived at the island office by 9:30 AM. This dedication was not new to me; it mirrored the commitment I had demonstrated during my time in the insurance industry.

Recruiting and training young marketers, many of whom were new to the real estate sector, became a source of joy and fulfillment. Each sale they made not only contributed to their growth but also to my success, both financially and professionally. This role significantly elevated my position as an authority figure within the team and among other realtors who interacted with our company.

The turning point came when Pascal Property rebranded to Blessed Homes. Inspired by the company's evolution and my growing influence, I made the decision to start my own subsidiary under Blessed Homes. By this time, I had built a robust team of over 80 members who were not only performing well but were also becoming mentors themselves in the real estate sector. This step marked a significant milestone in my journey, not just as a real estate consultant and salesperson but as a leader and shaping the future of the industry.

Under the aegis of the newly branded Blessed Group, I registered as Blessed

Real Estate Solutions, a dedicated real estate agency committed to selling and promoting only products and services offered by Blessed Homes. This alignment not only streamlined our operations but also significantly enhanced our brand's presence in the market. It was during this period that I achieved a landmark sales figure—59 million naira—an achievement that profoundly changed my professional and personal life.

My philosophy in business has always been centered on leveraging opportunities to their maximum potential. In the real estate industry, developers often set sales targets that come with enticing incentives, such as cars, home appliances, and more. I embraced these challenges wholeheartedly and succeeded in winning numerous incentives. Notably, I won my first car from Blessed Homes, a gesture that took me by surprise as the company had registered the vehicle under its name without my prior knowledge.

The success was not mine alone; several of my top team members also won cars, reflecting the overall effectiveness and motivation within our team. In 2021, my achievements caught the attention of former colleagues and bosses from the insurance industry. Those who had observed my transition and growth began reaching out for mentorship in real estate, recognizing the expertise and leadership skills I had developed.

That same year, the Managing Director of Blessed Group recognized the potential for further expansion and tasked me with recruiting more high-performing sales personnel. At this point, my team had grown to over 200 members. In response to this challenge, I began to recruit not only from within the real estate sector but also targeted experienced marketers and managers from the insurance industry. I introduced them to Blessed Group's ambitious 10-year operational vision. Despite the plan's ambitious nature, which some might consider unrealistic, I believed in it wholeheartedly. I instilled this belief in my team, teaching them to adopt and promote this vision with the same level of conviction.

This phase of my career was not just about personal growth but also about fostering a culture of success and aspiration among my team. By recruiting individuals who showed skills and competencies especially in sales, and mentoring them to achieve their best, I not only contributed to their professional development but also ensured the sustained growth and success of Blessed Real Estate Solutions within the competitive landscape of real estate.

As my role within the industry expanded and my responsibilities as a leader grew, I was struck by a profound realization about the importance of personal development. I recognized that to maintain my growth trajectory and meet the increasing demands of being perceived as an industry leader within the Real Estate , I needed to continuously evolve, both personally and professionally. This understanding led me to the insight that unlearning outdated practices and relearning new strategies were essential steps in sustaining success.

With the awareness that "Once you stop learning, you start dying," a quote by Albert Einstein, echoing in my mind, I felt a pressing need to deepen my knowledge formally. My quest for education was driven by the conviction articulated by Warren Buffett: "The best investment you can make is an investment in yourself. The more you learn, the more you'll earn." This belief fueled my search for academic and practical learning opportunities that could enhance my expertise in real estate.

In March 2021, while exploring various educational platforms online, I discovered the School of Estate. The timing was perfect, and the opportunity was precisely what I needed to advance my understanding of the Real Estate sector. I eagerly enrolled, committed to absorbing as much knowledge as possible. This decision to return to a structured learning environment was a strategic move to sharpen my skills and broaden my perspectives, ensuring that I could continue to lead and innovate in an industry that is constantly evolving.

The experience at the School of Estate was transformative. It not only provided me with advanced tools and techniques pertinent to real estate but also enriched my approach to business and leadership. This phase of my education reinforced the idea that continual learning is indispensable in the pursuit of excellence and leadership in any field, especially one as dynamic as real estate.

Embracing this path of continuous personal and professional development has allowed me to remain at the forefront of the industry, ready to tackle new challenges and seize opportunities with a well-informed and strategic approach. This commitment to education and growth has become a cornerstone of my philosophy as a leader and a pivotal part of my narrative as a real estate professional.

After completing rigorous training at the School of Estate, I continued my educational journey by getting certified as a fellow of the Institute of Management Consulting. This new qualification, combined with my background, equipped me to train my team and newcomers eager to learn about the real estate sector. I also started organizing investor hangouts to educate individuals on leveraging real estate for wealth creation.

My social media presence grew as I began hosting live sessions to educate investors and realtors about critical considerations in the real estate sector, whether as a realtor or an investor. Demonstrating my commitment to my teachings, I purchased my first land through Blessed Homes and Property, where I served as the MD of my own subsidiary in sales and marketing.

However, despite the success, a significant challenge arose. The General Managing Director (GMD) of Blessed Homes initiated a structural change by promoting my top sales team members to become MDs. This decision was made without prior communication and seemed to replicate the structure I had created for my subsidiary, leading to tension and discord within my team. Seeds of envy and discord sown by the group, coupled with my absence due to a commitment in Enugu, led to a breakdown within my team. By the time I returned, the situation had deteriorated significantly: key staff members had resigned and joined a competing company, leaving me devastated and physically unwell from the stress.

This period of hardship was compounded when my partnering company declared my top sales team as independent, effectively stripping me of my foundational support without notice. I found myself needing to rebuild from scratch, a task that seemed insurmountable as it coincided with a decline in my productivity and focus.

During this tumultuous time, I refocused on a micro thrift business I had started in 2018, initially to support my insurance customers. This Esusu (daily contribution) business, which I had developed into a fully Operational Enterprise in Agege, Lagos, became a dual-purpose office, also serving Real Estate inquiries. It was here that I began to reevaluate my strategy, realizing the importance of promoting my own brand rather than just my partner company's.

This shift in focus brought its own set of challenges. My decreased productivity did not go unnoticed, and I faced intense scrutiny and eventual punitive measures from my partnering company. When I refused to shut down my personal business as demanded, I was suspended indefinitely, and my car—a prize from my earlier successes but registered under the company's name—was seized. I was also barred from the company's premises and activities.

This moment was a turning point, emphasizing a crucial lesson: the importance of building and maintaining one's personal brand and assets independent of any partnerships. The ordeal taught me resilience and the need to always be prepared to stand alone if necessary, using the adversity as a stepping stone to forge a new path forward. As I navigated this challenging phase, I was guided by a renewed focus on self-reliance and the pursuit of a vision that was entirely my own, setting the stage for the next chapter in my professional life.

CHAPTER FOUR

LESSONS LEARNED SO FAR

Throughout my journey in the Real Estate sector, I have encountered numerous challenges and celebrated many victories. Each experience has taught me invaluable lessons about the industry, entrepreneurship, and personal growth. Here, I share these lessons and offer advice to those just starting their journey in real estate or any other entrepreneurial venture.

1. Education is Key: Never underestimate the power of continuous learning. My training at the School of Estate and becoming a certified management consultant significantly broadened my understanding and enhanced my skills. For those starting out, invest in your education—whether through formal schooling, workshops, or industry certifications. The more knowledgeable you are, the better equipped you'll be to handle the complexities of the market.

2. Focus on Building Your Brand: My experiences, especially the challenges with my former partnering company, highlighted the importance of building and promoting your own brand. It's crucial to develop a strong personal brand that can stand independently of any partnerships or affiliations. This ensures that in times of change or turmoil, your professional identity and business can continue to thrive.

3. Clear Communication is Crucial: One of the early mistakes I made was not clearly communicating terms regarding commissions which led to disputes. Always be transparent with clients, partners, and team members about all aspects of your business dealings. Clear communication prevents misunderstandings and builds trust, which is essential for long-term success.

4. Due Diligence Cannot Be Overlooked: The lesson learned from my first land sale, where I failed to perform adequate due diligence, was a tough one. Always verify every detail about the properties you handle, from legal status to physical condition. This not only protects you but also ensures that your clients are satisfied with their investments.

5. Embrace Leadership and Mentorship: As I grew my team and trained newcomers, I realized the importance of good leadership and mentorship. Being a great leader isn't just about directing others but inspiring and teaching them. For those stepping into managerial roles, remember that your team's growth contributes to your success.

6. Prepare for Adversity: Adversity is an inevitable part of any business. The challenges I faced, particularly the near-collapse of my team and the loss of my car, taught me the importance of resilience. Always have contingency plans and maintain a network of support to help navigate through tough times.

7. Protect Your Investments: Whether it's securing the legal rights to property or safeguarding business assets, always take steps to protect your investments. This includes ensuring that all business dealings are documented and legally sound, particularly when entering into partnerships.

8. Promote Independence Within Teams: Encouraging independence among team members can lead to innovation and growth. While it's important to provide guidance and support, also create an environment where team members can take initiative and develop their own skills.

9. Stay Ethical and Honest: Maintain a strong ethical foundation in all your dealings. Honesty not only fosters trust and loyalty among clients and colleagues but also builds a reputable and sustainable business.

10. Keep Faith and Stay the Course: Finally, maintain faith in yourself and your vision, even when faced with setbacks. My spiritual faith and the advice from my spiritual father were crucial in steering me through rough waters. Stay committed to your goals and remain flexible to adapt to changes.

These lessons have shaped me into the professional I am today. For those just starting out, remember that every challenge is an opportunity to learn and grow. Stay curious, be adaptable, and always strive for excellence.

11. Navigating a Male-Dominated Industry:

Being a woman in the real estate industry, a field predominantly occupied by men, presents a unique set of challenges. In this environment, my journey was not just about building a business; it was also about carving out a space where a woman's voice, insights, and leadership could be recognized and respected.

The real estate sector, like many others, often sets a default expectation of male leadership, influencing everything from networking opportunities to negotiation dynamics and decision-making processes. As a woman, breaking through these implicit barriers meant not only proving my competence but also challenging the subtle biases that can hinder access to critical resources and opportunities.

Key to navigating these challenges has been an ongoing commitment to self-love and personal development. Self-love in this context is about more than self-care; it's about self-respect, demanding fairness, and seeking recognition for my achievements and capabilities. It's also about setting boundaries that prevent burnout and ensuring that I am valued and respected within the industry.

Personal development has been equally crucial. Continual learning and improvement have enabled me to stay ahead in my field, bringing innovative ideas and solutions that distinguish my contributions from the norm. By gaining a deep understanding of the market, mastering new skills, and staying updated with industry trends, I've been able to position myself as a leader whose opinions and decisions are valued and respected.

Perhaps one of the most transformative aspects of my journey has been the strategic partnerships and friendships I've cultivated. In a male-dominated field, building alliances with both male and female colleagues who share similar values and goals has been invaluable. These relationships have provided mutual support, opened up new opportunities, and fostered a collaborative rather than competitive atmosphere.

Particularly noteworthy are my co-developers, Mr. Chris Emodi and Mr. Femi Oshonowro. Both have shown a remarkable inclination towards collaboration over competition, significantly enriching our projects with their expertise and shared vision for success. Their partnership has not only enhanced our developments but also reinforced the power of teamwork in overcoming industry challenges.

Moreover, the support from friends like Dr. Jennifer Seidu, who has been a pillar of encouragement from the inception of my career as a realtor, has been indispensable. Her belief in my abilities and her continuous support have played a crucial role in my professional growth and personal resilience.

The path has not been easy, but it has been incredibly rewarding. Through continuous self-love, personal development, and by forging strategic partnerships and friendships, I've been able to navigate the complexities of a male- dominated industry successfully, though, still learning the odds. Each step forward not only advances my career but also broadens the path for other women in real estate, making it a little easier for those who will follow. This journey has reinforced a crucial lesson: that true strength lies in resilience, learning, and the power of unity.

CHAPTER FIVE

KEEPING UP THE PACE

My journey has been punctuated with numerous struggles and adversities that have instilled in me a resolute belief: "No matter how hard life gets, I will never give up." This mantra isn't just a casual phrase but a guiding principle that I've prominently placed on my vision board, surrounded by other goals and aspirations

I aim to achieve. The departure from my previous partnering company marked a pivotal moment in my life, challenging me to commit fully to my path of success, regardless of the obstacles.

In the aftermath of leaving Blessed Homes and Properties, I found myself at a crossroads, uncertain of the exact steps to take but fueled by an unyielding determination to rise again. My clients, who over two years of hard work and diligence had grown to trust and believe in me, played a crucial role during this transitional phase. Some of these clients evolved into mentors, offering guidance as I navigated this new chapter.

The first concrete step I took was to establish my own Real Estate Firm. By this time, I had secured the necessary certificate of incorporation from the Corporate Affairs Commission and a license from EFCC through their Special Control Unit Against Money Laundering. With a modest capital of 1,800,000 Naira—all that remained of my savings after personal and professional investments—I rented an office space. Here, I took on multiple roles: Managing Director, Sales Officer, Accountant, Customer Service Representative, and Social Media Manager, while outsourcing graphic design to manage costs effectively.

An encounter with an old friend, who owned a real estate company, proved fortuitous. After earning a commission from selling properties for his firm, he offered me 20 plots of land in his estate. This transaction was instrumental in the foundation of my own real estate company, Klassickuewn Properties, which officially began operations on November 20th, 2021, from our office at 1 Anike Apena Street, Mobolaji Bank Anthony Way, Ikeja, Lagos.

With the support of another friend skilled in digital marketing, we developed a website to establish our online presence and reach a broader audience. These initial steps were critical, not just in setting up the business, but in signaling a fresh start—a rebirth of sorts from the trials that had previously beset me.

In the new office of Klassickuewn Properties, the setup was modest yet functional, tailored to my strengths and immediate needs. The front desk served as our operational hub, and the open space, filled with white plastic chairs, was designated for training—a domain I was intimately familiar with. Recognizing the need to expand my capabilities beyond training, I made a strategic decision to develop the human capital wing of Klassickuewn while gradually learning how to manage the real estate aspects of the business.

With a commitment to deepening my real estate knowledge, I revisited the educational materials from the School of Estate. This refresher was not merely academic; it sparked the creation of innovative real estate products tailored to the needs of our market. Concurrently, I transformed my existing esusu company into a real estate investment club. This strategic pivot repurposed our Agege office into a bustling retail hub for

Klassickuewn Properties, with our esusu clients becoming pivotal financial backers of our real estate ventures.

Encouragement from my clients bolstered my confidence in this new direction. A notable affirmation came from Mr. Iyoha Gabin, a client who inspired me with his words, "Peace, you can do this. If you can help your partner build, you can build yours." His belief in my capabilities was underscored by a significant investment of 2,000,000 naira for two years. Additionally, a friend who had designed our website facilitated another investment of 3,000,000 naira from one of his schoolmates. These investments were crucial in fully activating the operations of Klassickuewn Properties.

As the business began to attract more funds, I faced the challenge of allocating these resources effectively—a shift from my previous experience where funds were primarily used for loans or purchasing home appliances for clients at my micro thrift company. Recognizing the need for a robust financial management system, I brought on board our first accountant, Mr. Seun, in January 2022. His expertise was instrumental in harmonizing the financial transactions between the investment club and the real estate firm, and he established our inaugural accounting system.

Mr. Seun's contributions went beyond mere financial orderliness; they laid the groundwork for sustainable growth and compliance with financial regulations, ensuring that Klassickuewn Properties could withstand both current and future challenges. His role proved essential in transforming how we managed investments, setting a precedent for financial integrity and transparency within the company.

The journey of building Klassickuewn Properties from the ground up taught me the importance of adaptability, continuous learning, and strategic financial management. These early decisions and adjustments shaped the foundation of a business poised for growth and innovation in the competitive real estate market. As I reflect on these formative days, I am reminded of the power of perseverance, the impact of informed decision-making, and the value of supportive relationships in steering a nascent business toward long-term success.

As Klassickuewn Properties continued to flourish, the growth was not just in terms of financial success but also in the expansion of our team and client base. The office on Mobolaji Bank Anthony Way, once ample for our initial operations, began to feel increasingly cramped as both our staff strength and our team of in-house marketers grew. The physical constraints of our office space soon became a significant hurdle, making it clear that a larger environment was necessary to accommodate our expanding team and to maintain the productivity and comfort essential for continued success.

In response to this need, we began the search for a new office location that could support our growing operations and provide a conducive environment for our staff and clients. The move to a larger office was not just a logistical decision but also a strategic one, reflecting our broader vision for the company's future.

During this period of logistical growth, another challenge presented itself: our brand's global reach and recognition. We had successfully tapped into the diaspora market, attracting clients from various parts of the world. However, feedback indicated that the name Klassickuewn Properties Ltd was challenging for some international clients to connect with, potentially hindering our global appeal and marketing efforts.

To address these issues and to better encapsulate the expanding scope of our services—which now included Facility Management and Educational Services—we embarked on a rebranding initiative. In June 2023, Klassickuewn Properties Ltd was rebranded as Trusted Choice Assets Ltd. This new name was chosen to reflect the reliability, diversity, and quality of services we offered, resonating well with both local and international clients and aligning with our mission to provide trusted real estate solutions.

The rebranding process was comprehensive, involving not only a change of name but also a revamp of our corporate identity, marketing materials, and digital presence. This strategic transformation was aimed at reinforcing our position in the market as a versatile and dependable partner in real estate and related services.

The transition to Trusted Choice Assets Ltd marked a new chapter in our journey, symbolizing growth, adaptation, and our commitment to meeting the evolving needs of our clients. This change was met with positive responses from clients and partners alike, who appreciated the fresh identity and expanded offerings. It reinforced our dedication to not only grow as a company but to evolve in a way that continually serves the best interests of our clients and stakeholders.

The rebranding of Klassickuewn Properties to Trusted Choice Assets Ltd not only marked a transformation in our corporate identity and service offerings but also ignited a remarkable shift in our team dynamics. Among our staff, three members in particular—Chiamaka Ubani, Cletus Dumbiri, and Paul Sulaimon—

exemplified the positive impact of this change. These individuals, who were part of the organization prior to the rebranding, exhibited a renewed commitment and vigor post-rebranding that significantly contributed to the firm's momentum.

This newfound energy and dedication seemed to stem from the rebranding itself, which instilled a sense of ownership and pride among the staff. Chiamaka, Cletus, and Paul worked with a zeal that suggested the very life of the company depended on their efforts. Recognizing their invaluable contributions and leadership potential, we elevated their roles from regular staff members to top management positions. This elevation was not merely a change in title but a strategic move to empower them further and align their capabilities with the company's long-term vision.

The rebranding also catalyzed significant expansions and new ventures. One of the most notable achievements was the acquisition of our estate in Asaba—a strategic move that not only expanded our geographic footprint but also enhanced our portfolio significantly. This acquisition was a testament to our growing influence and capabilities in the real estate sector.

Building on this momentum, we established the South Estate Regional Office, located at 12 O.J Nnamani Crescent, Independence Layout. This new office was strategically positioned to manage our operations in the region and to serve as a hub for our expanding activities in the southern part of the country. The establishment of this regional office in 2024 underscored our commitment to providing localized and efficient services to our clients.

The impact of the rebranding and these strategic expansions was profound. Trusted Choice Assets Ltd quickly became recognized not only for the quality of its Real Estate solutions but also for its robust management team and strong regional presence. The transformations within the company reflected a clear alignment of our brand's values with our operational strategies, ensuring that we remained at the forefront of innovation and customer satisfaction in the real estate industry.

As Trusted Choice Assets Ltd continues to grow and adapt, the foundational changes implemented during this pivotal period will undoubtedly continue to influence and drive our success. The journey of rebranding and expansion has taught us the importance of flexibility, the value of a committed team, and the impact of strategic geographic and market expansion. These elements combined have set the stage for continued growth and success, establishing Trusted Choice Assets Ltd as a leader in the real estate sector.

As I reflect on the journey that has led me to this point, I am filled with a profound sense of gratitude and humility. From my humble beginnings, navigating the complexities of the insurance sector, to the creation and growth of Trusted

Choice Assets Ltd, each step along the way has been instrumental in shaping who I am today—not just as a businessperson, but as an individual committed to making a difference in the lives of others.

The path has not been without its challenges. There have been moments of doubt, setbacks that seemed insurmountable, and times when the weight of my dreams and responsibilities felt almost too heavy to bear. However, through each trial, I have learned that resilience, paired with a steadfast dedication to one's vision, is key to overcoming obstacles. The journey has taught me the power of perseverance and the importance of adapting to change while staying true to one's core values and goals.

To those who are at the beginning of their journey or are facing difficulties, let my story be a testament to the fact that no challenge is too great when faced with courage and determination. Embrace each setback as an opportunity to learn and grow. Remember, the most formidable barriers often hide the greatest opportunities for personal development and success.

The rebranding of our company was not just a change of name, but a rebirth that invigorated our team and expanded our horizons. It reminded us that transformation is a natural part of growth, and embracing change is essential to staying relevant and effective in meeting the evolving needs of those we serve.

The expansions into new regions and the development of new products were milestones that marked our progress not only in terms of business growth but also in our ability to impact more lives positively. These achievements are not mine alone but belong to every member of our team, our clients, and our supporters who have journeyed with us.

As we look to the future, I am excited about the possibilities that lie ahead. I am committed to continuing this journey with the same zeal and integrity that have brought us this far. For those reading this book, whether you are a budding entrepreneur, a seasoned professional, or someone simply seeking inspiration, I encourage you to hold fast to your dreams. Be bold in your aspirations, diligent in your actions, and unwavering in your commitment to excellence.

Thank you for sharing this journey with me. Let us continue to strive for success, not just for ourselves but for the betterment of our communities and the world at large. Together, let us build legacies that will endure and inspire generations to come.

CONCLUSION

As I close this chapter of my story, I do so knowing that each page turned has been a step toward a greater understanding of not only business but also life. I've come to see that entrepreneurship is more than the pursuit of financial success; it's a journey of personal transformation and a test of one's values and convictions.

Looking back, I see that the moments of true growth came not from the successes but from the hardships that tested my resolve. These experiences have ingrained in me a deeper sense of purpose and a clearer vision of the kind of leader I aspire to be—one who empowers, educates, and uplifts others.

The evolution of our company from Klassickuewn Properties to Trusted Choice Assets Ltd has been a metaphor for my own transformation. It is a reminder that identities, whether personal or corporate, are not fixed but are continually evolving. This adaptability has been crucial in navigating the ever-changing landscapes of the markets we serve and in responding to the needs of our clients with agility and foresight.

In sharing my story, my hope is that it serves not just as a narrative of success, but as a source of inspiration and a roadmap for others. To those who dream of carving out their own path in the world, know that while the journey will demand resilience and courage, it is also filled with the potential for extraordinary achievement and personal fulfillment.

Let this book be a reminder that every challenge faced and every obstacle overcome adds to the richness of your journey. Embrace each experience, learn from each failure, and celebrate each victory. And through it all, stay true to your values, for they will guide you when the path becomes uncertain.

To my readers, remember that the journey is as important as the destination. The relationships you build, the knowledge you gain, and the integrity you maintain are the true measures of success. Keep pushing forward, keep striving for greatness, and keep believing in the power of your dreams.

Thank you for walking this path with me through the pages of this book. May your journeys be filled with courage, hope, and unwavering determination. Let us move forward together, building not just businesses, but lives filled with purpose and a world enriched by our contributions.

ABOUT THE AUTHOR

Peace Ukamaka O. is a dynamic entrepreneur, author, and the Managing Director of Trusted Choice Assets Ltd, a pioneering force in 21st-century real estate. With over half a decade of specialized experience in Marketing and sales, Peace is renowned for her expertise in sales consultancy, coaching, and innovative marketing strategies.

Peace's business journey began in 2016 as a Sales Representative at Mutual

Benefit Life Assurance. Her exceptional skills quickly elevated her to Unit Manager at African Alliance Insurance Plc. As a serial entrepreneur, Peace introduced groundbreaking financial solutions, such as the 'Ajo' banking model, empowering underserved communities within the insurance and banking sectors.

Over the years, Peace has partnered with more than 50 licensed real estate firms across Nigeria, guiding over 500 clients through successful real estate ventures. Her mission is to address Nigeria's housing deficit by empowering individuals to make informed real estate decisions. A distinguished alumna of School of Estate Batch 46 and a Fellow of the Institute of Management Consultants (IMC/CMC), Peace also serves as the Principal of the Nigeria Training Institute of Real Estate Entrepreneurs (NIRE).

Peace is deeply committed to human capital development, having mentored and empowered over 1,000 individuals and counting. Her visionary goal is to cultivate 10,000 self-made millionaires in the real estate industry. She also hosts the weekly radio show "Real Estate Matter," conducts impactful seminars, and leads training sessions that offer actionable, real-world solutions.

In 2023, Peace was honored with the CEO/Founder of the Year award by TIBA (The Iconic Brand Award), recognizing her significant contributions to the real estate industry. Additionally, she was recently appointed as a West

Africa Youth Ambassador by the West Africa Youth Council, a testament to her influence and commitment to empowering the next generation.

As an accomplished author, Peace has penned several influential books, including "Who Are You?", "50 Common Mistakes New Realtors Must Avoid," "Understanding Real Estate Laws and Regulations," and "Team Building: The Money-Making Machine." These publications have become essential resources for professionals in sales, marketing, and business development.

Ready to elevate your career and achieve your goals? Connect with @peaceukamaka across social media platforms or via email at officialpeaceukamaka@gmail.com. Join her on a transformative journey where innovation meets expertise, and dreams become reality.

www.ingramcontent.com/pod-product-compliance
Lightning Source LLC
Chambersburg PA
CBHW050327230526
45471CB00005B/2391